Stronger Together

By
G E Bates

Grosvenor House
Publishing Limited

This book is published by
Grosvenor House Publishing Ltd
Link House
140 The Broadway, Tolworth, Surrey, KT6 7HT.
www.grosvenorhousepublishing.co.uk

A CIP record for this book
is available from the British Library

Paperback ISBN 978-1-83615-386-3

DEDICATIONS

This book is dedicated to my Husband,
children and grandchildren.

Firstly to my Husband, JOHN ANDREW BATES, who
has put up with so much from me but still loved me
enough to be my rock when i was unsteady, the light in
my darkest times, my soul mate, safe space and my
happy place. This man is the most supportive,
inspirational and selfless man any woman could wish to
be married to and I am truly blessed to call myself his
wife. Thankyou Mr Husband, for showing me that love
isn't in what we say but is in everything we do.

To my Son, COREY-JOHN ANDREW BATES (C-J)
our tiger cub, who has become a fine young man, who
wears his heart on his sleeve, which can be a blessing
and a curse. When he loves, he loves hard and when he
hurts, he hurts brutally but he is the most kind and
caring young man any mum could wish for and I am so
proud to call him my son. when he laughs, the sun
shines, thank you C-J for showing us that despite the
struggles and challenges we face, how to not let it get us
down but instead, keep our heads held high, thankyou
for bringing the sunshine into our lives.

For our Daughter, SASHA LAURA LOUISE BATES,
our Angel, I often think she had it the toughest, there

are so many moments I wish I could go back to and do differently, but in spite of everything, she made it! she is smart, funny and incredibly independent but most of all, she is the most amaaaazing mum, who knows how to love deeply. Thankyou Angel, for showing me that I dont have to be afraid to make decisions without the aid of outside influences and reminding me that making mistakes is ok as long as you own it. Angel, you are a blessing and to call you my daughter is nothing short of an honour, thankyou for showing me what the unconditional love of a mother truly is.

To our Daughter, PHOEBE-ROSE STELLA BATES, our Angel girl, she is our fire cracker in a tornado, she's not afraid to say whats on her mind, phoebe knows what she wants... and usually gets it. She couldn't care less about what others think and once her mind is set, there's no changing it, but even with this hard exterior, she also has a heart of gold and is incredibly funny, she adores our furbabies and will openly tell you she much prefers them to humans, I am sooo blessed to call her my daughter. Angel girl, thankyou for making me laugh so much with your wicked one liners, for showing me how to see the positives in everything and how to not care what others think.

To all three of you, thank you all for being brutally honest when I've needed it, for loving me despite my flaws but most of all for giving me a second chance to be the mum I wish I had been, the mum I never knew I could be and the mum you all truly deserve.

For our Grandchildren, firstly RENESME OLIVIA TAYLOR, our little Angel, for a two year old you have this larger than life attitude with a killer death stare, it's impossible to be sad with you around, you are already a determined little soul, you keep being you little A and don't change for anyone, and for our Grandson, MADDOX NOAH TAYLOR, our little Smiler, your many smiles and little giggles melt my heart, at 5 months old you are already showing signs of a cool, calm and collected, beautiful human and i know that as u continue to grow your light will only shine brighter. You have both brought so much joy and love into our lives, I feel so blessed and honored to be your Nana, every moment spent with you both is so precious, I will always treasure every memory we make together. Thankyou both for the joy you have brought into my life and for helping me to let go of the fears that I have carried with me for way too long.

I would also like to mention my son in law JOSHUA TAYLOR and daughter in law ZOE DIXON, you are both very special people and I'm so proud to have you as part of our family, wanting to be part of our crazy family makes you equally as crazy and therefore perfect fits l.o.l. seriously though, thankyou both for loving Sasha and C-J like they so deserve to be loved.

ACKNOWLEDGEMENTS

To my Mum and Dad, **DAVID AND LAURA ANDERSON,** Thank you for all you have both done for me, I know it hasn't been an easy ride but, as the great parents you are, you didn't give up and I will always be grateful for that. Thank you for showing me that giving up is not an option.

To my awesome little sister, **EMMA LOUISE PARKER (nee Anderson),** You took me and C-J in soooo many times during my first marriage, even when I went back and things went bad again and again, you always opened your door to us, even when you had your own problems and your own son to raise, it didn't stop you caring enough to help us, I will be forever grateful to you for everything you did for us back then and in all the years that followed.

To my amazing in laws, **STELLA BATES, GEORGE BATES, MARG BATES, MATTHEW BATES, MAZ BATES** and the honorary sister in law, **ZOE ATKINSON** and her partner **PHIL COLBERT,** as in laws go, they are definitely not the stereotypical monster in laws often depicted in films, I couldn't ask for better, more fun, caring and most loyal in laws then these awesome human beings, who have stood by us and helped when we've needed. Thankyou for making me feel like part of the family and for being the best in laws a person could wish for, I am so blessed to have you all in my life.

STELLA - you as a mother in law have given me so much joy and many reasons to laugh especially when I've been down, you also gave me the most precious gift of all, the beautiful soul that is your son you have also been the most amazing nan to the kids, with you they have had so much fun, so much love and many beautiful memories to treasure. thankyou for everything.

MAZ - You have been there for us right from the start, you have supported us, both physically and emotionally and you've always stood by us, and the laughs we've had... oh the laughs haha. you've always made me feel like I can come to you for and with anything, I really couldn't ask for a better sister in law. thank you for all you've done for us, it has meant more then you'll ever know.

ZOE AND PHIL - Zoe you looked after CJ for us on more than one occasion, when we needed it most but you were also there for the rest of us, supporting us all in our times of need, you are one of the most compassionate people i have ever had the pleasure of knowing and Phil thank you so much for all the help you gave John when we needed, it meant alot, thank you both so much for all you've done and the love you've given, we are truly blessed to have you in our lives.

To my brother **STEVE GOW** and my sister in law **JO GOW,** you have both been there when I've needed you,

you always have my back, you believe in me and you force me to believe in myself. You don't take any crap from anyone and you have shown me I don't need to either. Bro, when you and John get together we belly laugh until we ache so Thank you for the laughs, for being the most amazing godfather to C-J and also for looking out for John and the girls too, Jo thank you for dropping your own stuff to come sit with me when I've been down, you're amazing and i can see why my brother loves you. I am so blessed to have you both in my life, Thank you for teaching me and forcing me to repeat that one line that helps get me past all the negativity... "I don't give a fuck" I love you both!

To my amazingly wonderful girls. my soul sisters, **LISA SANDERS, ELIANE FAKHOURY TAMMY PHILLIPS AND JAYNE ROBERTS,** all of whom have comforted me in my dark times, laughed with me when I've needed the giggles, had shoulders to cry on when I couldn't hold it together and all been the mad heads I know and love. Thank you all for showing me there are still genuinely good, loyal and trustworthy people in this world, I couldn't be more honoured to have you all in my life and I couldn't wish for better friends, the kind of friends that I'm not afraid to call family.

To my godparents **KAY THOMAS AND PAUL THOMAS** and godalogical sisters, **KELLY BOWERS, FRANCESCA DAVIES AND DANIELLE THOMAS,** all of whom knew when something was seriously wrong and chose to stand by us without a second thought, for this we are forever greatful and have so much love for each and every one of you, to have such wonderful godparents and amazing godalogical sisters is a true blessing thankyou for wanting to be a part of our lives.

JOHN AND RACHEL PROBERT what can I say, right from the get go you had John's back through one of the darkest times of our lives, you welcomed him and looked out for him, giving him the truest friendship a guy could have, then I came along to pick him up one day and you welcomed me too, Rachel you really do make a damn fine brew haha, we are truly blessed to have you in our lives, thankyou for welcoming us and being the friends most people could only ever dream of having.

Finally, to my big sister (who ironically is shorter then me l.o.l) **LISA MARIE WAKE** (nee Anderson), Author of **LOVE, HOPE AND COMFORT, MY ANXIETY AND ME** and **THE LOVE WITHIN A GRATEFUL HEART.** who has shown me that it's always possible to follow and achieve your dreams, Thankyou for being my inspiration and giving me the push I needed to realise my own dreams and make them happen.

I WANT TO THANK EACH AND EVERY ONE OF YOU FOR BEING A SPECIAL PART OF MY LIFE, I FEEL TRULY BLESSED AND SO ENRICHED, I AM A BETTER PERSON FOR KNOWING YOU ALL AND HAVING YOU ALL IN MY LIFE. THANKYOU. XXX

CONTENTS

AN IMPORTANT MESSAGE

Life can throw so much at us and it can get really tough but we can let it drag us down or we can choose to fight for ourselves and the ones we love.

People will come and go from our lives, friends, some of which will leave due to disagreements, others just drift away, and the ones that stay, we can be fortunate to consider as family, Then there are the family members who also come and go, for the same reasons, and it's important to know that blood doesn't make you family, it makes you related, sharing DNA doesn't make you obligated to love them especially if all they do is drag you down. Family isn't about the blood that runs through your veins its about the love that flows through your heart.

Surrounding yourself with those who choose to stand by you through good times and bad, who will forgive your mistakes and who will listen without judgement, that is family.

I watched an episode of 9.1.1 and one of the characters, Henrietta "Hen" Wilson had this monologue that totally embodies the essence of the poems in this book,

"Life hits you head on sometimes, there is always going to be pain and the fallout that comes with it, sometimes it feels like the universe is out to get you but maybe it's just trying to get your attention, we can spend our days trying to understand the pain and we should, it's how we heal but we must always remember, it's not the trauma that defines us, it's how we choose to react to it"

The poems in this book are largely based on survival, hope and love, it's these things we should carry with us always because no matter what life throws, no matter what we have to endure, there is always light at the end of the tunnel, there is always hope, there is always love and having the right kind of support can only make us stronger as individuals and Stronger Together.

STRONGER THAN YOU THINK

"Oh wow, what did you do?"
"This? it's nothing, just a bruise"
"but how did you get it?"
"silly really, I slipped"

Excuse after excuse, time and again,
how much longer can this go on?
He promised he'd stop, wont do it again,
but he'll do it again before long.

His hand around my thoat, "I need money"
"please stop, I dont have any"
"then go ask them"
"I can't, not again, I wont"
"you know what will happen if you don't"

Thrown to the floor, he grips my hair,
I try to push him away,
my head connects with the concrete floor,
one, two, three, blackout,
on the floor, almost lifeless I stay.

Slowly I open my eyes,
He's just sat at my feet, like he cares,
pulling his head from his hands, he turns to face me,
and all he can do is stare.
Blood drips from my mouth, tears stream down my
    face,

I crawl up the stairs to my baby,
He tries using force to get me to stay,
"If you think you can leave then you're crazy"

Many times I left, many times I returned,
always thinking things would be better,
but always being burned.
Controlled by his fists, controlled by his charm,
he always had me believing,
I'd no longer come to any harm.
His words just as lethal, mentally breaking me down,
Feeling nothing but fear and unnerved,
"You're a failure, worthless, useless to all"
This life is all I deserved.

but life has its way of sending you,
who or what you need,
To show you that you deserve way more,
to grab your hand and take the lead.
To build you up, To give you strength,
To help you find your courage,
To, once and for all, walk away
from that life of pain and suffrage.

It's really tough to walk away,
the aftermath is bloody rough too,
but with the right support and belief in yourself,
there isn't anything you can't get through.
You are strong, brave and worth way more than this,
believe in these words, they are true,
Just reach out for that guiding hand,
because a better life is waiting for you.

HAUNTED

His eyes haunt me,
Once they were filled with the joys of fatherhood
Then all at once sorrow,
We would never know our unborn child.

All I want is to carry his child,
My wretched body useless to help,
The uncertainty of another would tear me apart,
As I look into his eyes I'm crushed by his pain,
Like the ocean crashing against the walls of my heart,
The thunderous rain beats down on my mind
And the lightning strikes at my weakest point...
    my womb.

We keep trying with no luck, the pain to much to bear,
Thoughts take over my mind like a storm that grips the
    Earth,
Everywhere I look, babies, pregnant women,
I seek shelter in his soul
But his eyes haunt me,
For deep inside, our unborn child lives in his mind,
    in his heart,
There's nowhere to turn, no escape,
For the child we will never know and the child we may
    never have,
His eyes haunt me.

G E BATES

As I turn to my child from a life of the past,
Not his biologically but his where it counts,
The father within him takes over his body
As I watch them together, a father with his son.
A family bonded in love, I know we will survive,
For somewhere in the depths of the storm is a calm.

Dedicated to my Husband, JOHN BATES, who has
proved that being a Dad isn't about the blood that runs
through your veins, but the love that flows through
your heart.

SCRAMBLED THOUGHTS

I lay in bed, staring at a blank page,
My pen at the ready yet my hand is still,
So much running through my mind,
I close my eyes not knowing where to start.

Thoughts scream through my head,
Very soon I'm paralysed by my emotions,
Anger, frustration, grief, fear and pain,
Why them, so young, brought into this world
    and forgotten,
Why him he tries so hard,
What can I do, there's nothing I can do,
Why is this happening to us?

I can feel the tears stream down my face,
Stop now, please stop, open your eyes.
How do I protect them, please someone
    hear my voice,
Will we ever have the baby we dream of?
Is he Ok, it must be so hard for him?
Does anyone really understand?
Please stop, I can't breathe,
So much torment, so much pain,
Don't want to think anymore, don't want to
    feel anymore,
Please just open your eyes...

I look around the room,
It seems a little brighter than before,
My thoughts just a whisper, I look down,
My page no longer blank, my hand no longer still.

DANCING IN HEAVEN

We cannot know how you look right now,
How brown your hair, how blue your eyes,
We cannot feel your tiny hands
As you squeeze our fingers, trying to take a bite,
We cannot hear you call our names,
Or see your cheeky smile,
Yet all of these things we see in you,
When we picture you dancing in heaven.

As the years go by, you grow in our thoughts
And we think of all the little things,
Your first step taken, your first word spoken,
What joy to hold you would bring.
Taken from deep within, not destined for this world,
You live in our hearts and in our minds
As we think of you dancing in heaven.

Though you left before we met,
We are never far apart,
Nothing to remember but never forgotten,
You've truly touched our hearts.
Our tears may fall but our minds are at ease
For it's true we will meet someday,
How blessed we will be for eternity,
With our angel, dancing in heaven.

Dedicated to Jessica... the daughter we never got to
meet but will love deeply forever. 24-10-2005.

MOVING ON

I'm not going, I'm not going,
I want to stay where I am,
I know honey but you can't,
It's all part of growing up,
I don't want to grow up, it's not fair,
I'll miss all of my friends,
I'm sure you'll see them out and about,
And you'll make new ones, you'll be ok.
I'm scared, don't make me go,
I'll be with you every step of the way.

No longer the baby I held in my arms,
That precious day he was born,
A lump in my throat,
Tears come and go,
The next stage of his life draws near,
A last performance, disco and leavers assembly,
As they prepare to go their separate ways,
The day finally comes to bid farewell to his friends,
As they part for new adventures.

The flood gates refuse to stay closed,
As the tears fall for days and days,
If only i could turn back time,
He could stay for a bit longer,
No worries of missing his friends,
Or even growing up,

But then what good would it do, to turn
    back time,
We would only be right here again.

I'm going, I'm going, I know I can't stay,
It's all part of growing up,
I'll miss all my friends, but with new ones I make,
I know I'll be Ok.
As scared as I am, I know one thing for sure,
I've got all of my family around me,
And there they will be, walking right beside me,
Every step of the way.

Dedicated to my son.. Corey-John Andrew who knows
his struggles but challenges himself regardless.

LOST AND FOUND

So quiet and sad, our little girl lost,
For the life she once had, our little girl lost,
A need to be wanted, but lets no-one in,
She does not dare love, can't even stand cuddling.

A barrier built up by a child so small,
A wall to tear down as many tears do fall,
For a lost little girl who cannot see,
We will fight for, find and love unconditionally.

Brick by brick, piece by piece,
Year by year, the heartache will seize,
Day by day the hugs grow strong,
Her heart opens and she knows now,
This is where she belongs,
Wanted, needed and loved beyond measure,
Our hearts belong to this little treasure.

Years now passed, no lost little girl I see,
Instead a strong young woman stands before me,
Her heart is big, her love knows no bounds,
There she is, our pride and joy,
A true love found.

Dedicated to my daughter... Sasha Laura Louise, who
has overcome so much and become the strongest most
loving young woman I could ever have hoped for.

REFLECTION OF A FIRECRACKER

She's the firecracker in a tornado,
You can't argue with her, you won't win,
There's nothing you can say that she cannot spin,
She can stump you with a single, spoken line,
She can give you a death stare one minute,
And the next she's fine.
No longer a little girl with curls in her hair,
Nor a cute little voice and plenty of hugs to share,
Instead, she sits in her room all alone,
Caring not for the thoughts of others,
Only the thoughts of her own.
When she looks in the mirror
She sees, not what we see,
But imperfections on a reflection
That won't leave her be.
It matters not what we think,
Only what she believes in her heart,
Our opinions differ greatly,
They couldn't be further apart,
But for the record, I'll tell you what it is we find,
A strong young woman, not afraid to speak her mind.
She knows what she wants and she usually gets it,
She's also not afraid to say "oh sh..ut up, I just wanna
    sleep for a bit".
But even with an exterior that seems so hard and cold,
What we can see is a beautiful young woman with a
    heart of gold.

She's incredibly funny, with brilliant one liners
And she will give everything a positive spin,
I just hope one day, she begins to see
The true beauty her reflection hides within.

Dedicated to my daughter - Phoebe-Rose Stella, who's strength, determination and positivity never ceases to amaze me.

AUTUMN ANGEL

As we light a candle for the one we did not know,
Only in our hearts and minds can our Autumn Angel
    grow,
Though you left before we met all those years before,
We can only imagine what life would have been like,
Had you been here for us to adore.
Now eighteen years have passed us by
And still we think of you,
We celebrate what could have been,
On the day we knew you were due.
So happy heavenly eighteenth birthday,
To the child we didn't get to know,
But we take comfort in knowing, that in our hearts
    and minds,
There will always be a place for our Autumn Angel to
    grow.

STORMS OF FREEDOM

A dark cloud, a thousand sorrows,
The pouring rain, a thousand tears,
A split second flash, a thousand openings
To the thunderous roar, a thousand fears.

A glimmer of light, warmth burns through,
The tears begin to slow,
The storms subside, the air freshens
And hope begins to grow.

The sun now bright, there's a joyous glow
And a sense of new beginnings,
A look, a smile and a sigh of relief
To see the lives we hold dear are blooming.

Though the clouds will darken our days
The sun has a secret to share,
For a brighter future where our flowers grow free
The storms come to clear the air.

FINDING PEACE

I don't know who i am,
No idea who I'm expected to be,
Pulled in every direction,
I'm lost in a world of emotion.
I'm a Mother, I'm a Wife,
I'm a Sister, I'm a Friend,
Do I really exist as me?

A heart that is filled with loved ones,
The joy that their laughter brings,
Shot down by the power of torment,
Outside influences pulling the strings,
Why is it nothing can be done,
Until all is at the brink,
So much agony and pain again and again,
Much more and we're likely to sink.

A struggle to keep us together,
As others try to tear us apart,
Like sharks in the depths of the ocean,
Just waiting to rip through our hearts.
I look on as they play by the shore,
Like angels they skip through the waves,
A sense of peace flows through me
And my worries drift away.

As cousins they came together,
As siblings they will unite,
Thoughts that their lives could be normal,
Dreams that they'll be alright.
A Mother, a Wife, a Sister, a Friend,
Do I really exist as me?
I know one day I'll find who I am,
And not who I'm expected to be.

MOMENT IN TIME

A moment in time,
A world dressed in white,
Alone on a hill,
Nothing to do but wait.

A pain stricken body
Sits where it fell,
Numbed by the freezing temperatures
Of the early morning air.

Minutes felt like hours
As I shivered from the cold
But relief came,
His voice calling my name.

Fighting his way up the snow covered hill,
Slipping with every other step,
He's soon by my side, checking I'm ok
Before sending me on my way.

As I glance back, he's smiling at me
And that's the moment in time when i knew,
Whenever I needed, in times good or bad,
He'd always be there for his little girl.

For my dad - David Anderson who has always worked
so hard to give his children what they need, the dad
every daughter deserves.

UNCONDITIONAL

When the tears fall, the rivers come
You know she will cry with you,
When you're feeling down and need a smile
You know she will smile at you,
When your days are dark and you can't see the light
You know she will find it for you,
When your struggle to fight is all but gone
She will put that fight back in you.

Down but never beaten
She rises to any challenge,
Putting others before herself,
Never asking for anything in return.
Always there to hold your hand
When times are looking bad,
The advice she gives is to the point,
Given with the loving heart she has.

When the tears fall, the rivers come
She knows you will cry with her,
When she's feeling down and needs a smile
She knows you will smile at her,
When days are dark and she can't see the light
She knows you will find it for her,
When her struggle to fight is all but gone
You will put that fight back in her.

Not a thing they won't do for one and other,
Love in its truest form,
For a mother and child, the love they share
Is unconditional.

For my mum – Laura Anderson, the sensitive soul who put her whole heart into motherhood.

FORGET TO REMEMBER

Hi Nana, how are you?
I'm sorry dear, but who are you?
It's me Nana, your granddaughter,
Of course you are, I'm no fool, would you like a brew?
I went in the garden today and sat in the sun,
Oh how lovely Nana, that sounds like fun,
I went in the garden today and sat in the sun,
Did you really Nana, that's great,
It's nice out there now spring has begun,
I went in the garden today and sat in the sun,
Aww that's nice Nana, I bet that was fun,
I'm sorry dear, but who are you?
It's me Nana, your granddaughter,
Of course you are, I'm no fool, would you like a brew?

To know you are lost somewhere deep in their mind,
Only ever to be found from time to time,
To have someone love you so, so much,
Look at you but not see you,
They forget who you are and look confused,
At all the things you say and do,
Repeated conversations, spoken as if for the first time,
Because you don't want them thinking they're losing
    their mind.
Frustrated, exhausted and full of despair,
Because one day they wander away,
They get lost, can't find their way home,
A fear of them being all on their own,

You find them and see they're confused and distressed,
You know their mind must be such a mess.
It matters not that they have forgotten your name,
Or that they repeat conversations over and over again,
What matters most is their happiness and safety,
Showing them your love, kindness and empathy,
You take the time to show them you care,
And let them know you'll always be there.

Nana, hey Nana, let's go home,
You shouldn't be out here all alone,
I'm sorry dear, but do I know you?
Yes Nana it's me, your granddaughter,
Of course you are, I'm no fool, would you like to come,
    have a brew?
Sure Nana, that would be nice,
And Nana, just want you to know... that I love you.

For my beautiful Nan - Julia Moreliegh loved and missed
always.

KNOWING YOU

I wish i'd have known you in your life
I know I would have loved you,
your home filled with the smell of fresh baked bread
and the smell of sweet jams too,
the sound of the radio, a notebook filled with cricket
    scores,
and lets not forget the football,
A home filled with laughter and plenty of fun,
With board games and darts down the hall.

In the magic circle and all its events,
it's you who'd feed all that would go,
As a cowgirl you danced, you so loved to dance,
you could really put on a good show.
Holidays with your family,
Arcades and ball games with your boys,
Your impressive shots on the crazy golf course,
It all gave you so much joy.

And as you sit on the bench by the river,
you release a contented sigh,
There's a smile on your face and peace in your heart,
watching the boats go by.

Such a strong and courageous person,
who truly enjoyed life,
A special woman with the kindest heart,
A loving mom and a beautiful wife.

Above all else, nothing means more to you,
Then that of your family,
and a promise you made, no matter where you are,
by their side you always would be.

Although I didn't know you in life,
I feel I know you well,
through your son that is my father,
And the stories he did tell.

So much you and I have in common,
so much you once loved I love too,
I love the thought that although we never met,
I could be just like you.

A special bond I feel between us
As our two worlds do colide,
the barrier between life and death broken,
Now i feel you walk by my side.

I wish I'd have known you in your life,
but I'm blessed to know you now, and it's true,
with a bond between us, forever held in my heart,
I can say with certainty, Dear Nan, I love you.

For my Nan ELIZABETH ANDERSON (NEE GAFF)

The Nan I never knew but who will always have a
special place in my heart.

OUR MATRIARCH

She's the brightest moon in the darkest night sky,
She's the sun, shining on a cloudy day,
She marches to the beat of her own drum,
She lets nobody stand in her way.

She's a pocket rocket, firey and fun,
She pulls her grandkids, on quilts down the stairs,
She'll have wheel barrow races, she loves to bake,
She's a feeder because she cares.

Christmas she loves, her house a grotto
and all for her family,
For her family, to her, is what means most,
Without them who would she be.

With a heart of gold, she's a beautiful soul
She would help anyone in need,
She'd give the clothes off her back or her very last
    pound,
She's the best of the best indeed,
but the sweetest thing about this woman,
The thing i most adore,
She has know idea just how special she is
and how much she's loved and cared for.

With a larger then life personality,
She's the heart of the family and shes truly left her
    mark,
 No words can describe how blessed we all are,
To have her as our Matriarch.

For my mother in law STELLA BATES.

You are more special then you know. xx

BORROWED

There's a feeling of emptiness
As we drive down the winding roads,
Raindrops fall on the screen in front,
Although the music plays,
An eerie silence takes hold,
I gaze at the sullen clouds and misted hills
And I wonder, is this it?

A father of a friend I'd made
All those years ago,
A father who I came to love
As if he was my own,
Defending me when times were bad,
With open arms came comfort,
He made me laugh but now i cry,
For gone is my borrowed dad.

His illness came as a shock,
These things, they don't happen to us,
But as time passed, we could not deny
He would soon be taken from us.
So much warning yet still not prepared
As we gathered to say goodbye,
So funny right till the end,
Though sometimes through no fault of his own,
He made us laugh but now we cry,
For gone is our borrowed dad.

My tears fall, my heart aches
And I can barely breath,
As I am left to wonder,
If he knew what he meant to me.
As the sky darkens,
And day turns to night,
Reality dawns, a believers truth,
Our time on Earth is borrowed, eternal life awaits,
And though his time has come to an end,
The imprint he's left in our lives,
Can only be matched by our love,
Sealed forever within his heart.

Dedicated to the man who tret me like one of his own —My Borrowed dad JAMES "Jim-Bob" GOW 28/08/1953 – 23/09/2008.

Loved and Missed Always!

A BEAUTIFUL LOVE

Love is beautiful, love is true!
Love is knowing the imperfections,
It is loving the imperfections.
Love knows and feels fear and pain,
It knows the mistakes we make again and again,
But love sees and understands,
It may bring trials and struggles, but it also brings
    helping hands.

It is true love comes in many forms,
The fast beating of hearts as you catch each others eye,
It's nerves that feel like butterflies,
It's two coffee cups now instead of one,
It's one toothbrush placed next to another,
It's the sign your future has begun.

Love is the light that shines in the darkness,
It's one catching the other if they fall,
Love is the glow that radiates,
As you stand side by side, standing tall,
Love brings two hearts together to beat as one,
It also brings miracles you thought not possible,
And a happiness that will not be undone.

Love is helping each other in good times and bad,
It's all the fun you ever wanted and all the fun you ever
    had,
Love comes in many forms,
It is beautiful and it's true,
For all these things and so much more,
Love comes in the form of you!

YOU WERE THERE

You were there to view our first house
   with us,
Down here in spud lane,
You were there to calm my nerves at darts,
When I began playing.
You were there as my right hand woman,
As we drunkenly stumbled to get our trophies,
Although i would certainly argue,
That you were more drunk then me.
You were there to make me belly laugh,
During our sleepovers...minus the sleep,
Now buckle up treacle,
Because here's where it gets deep!

You were there with forgiveness when i fucked up
   royally,
You were there when my world imploded,
And I felt I could trust nobody,
And when my own blood turned against me,
You were there standing by me,
With love, understanding and loyalty.

And what i know is as true as can be,
None of these are the actions of a friend,
But are the actions of those
The heart calls family.

Dedicated to my amazing friend **LISA SANDERS** who has been there for me though it all, she is the definition of true loyalty, true friendship and a true sisterhood.

BONDED HEARTS

At the heart of us all stands a woman so strong,
Giving life to us all, showing us a place we belong,
Bringing us together, with passion, love and loyalty,
She shows us the meaning of a blessed family.
Her beautiful heart accepts us for who we are,
Whether we are near or whether we are far,
But sometimes, just sometimes, she might well break,
Leaving her vulnerable for negativity to take,
But know this now, as we stand strong,
Side by side, we all have a shoulder
On which you can cry on,
So take our hands and know this to be true,
You've truly blessed our lives,
So please, see yourself as we see you,
The heart of us all, our teacher, our friend,
Our soul sister, whose love is without end,
Thus the reason, our gift to you,
support, devotion and loyalty too,
A bond and blessings that hold us together,
A family, not blood, but a family forever!

For my soul sister **ELIANE FAKHOURY** my crazy gal
who carries only love hope and peace in her heart,
blessing all who come into contact with her, a blessing
I am forever thankful for.

PEACE BY PIECE

When your head's filled with thoughts
Of all that's gone wrong,
When facing the uncertainty
Of all that's to come,
The ugliness of some drag you down,
Until you feel alone, your own mind almost gone,
When their pieces don't fit yours
But where else is there to belong,
When your mind is in chaos and it's hard to see
Through all of the confusion and negativity,
It's time to reach out to each piece of your puzzle,
To all that truly comforts through your torturous
    struggle,
Each flower that blooms, the light of the moon,
The wind that blows, birds singing their tune,
The loving dog that cuddles into you,
When you're in pain or feeling blue,
Each friend with a smile and a hand stretched out,
Each family member that shows what true love is
    about,
Each and every piece is the perfect fit,
All are connected with love,
And willing you not to quit.
They offer a place you can truly belong,
Where negativity and judgement will cease,
And for every right piece you find in your life,
You will also find strength, love and peace.

I MISS YOU

Not siblings by blood,
But through time and love,
In every way that matters
You are my little bruv.
You always had my back,
You always stood by me,
Our special sibling bond,
Was plain for all to see.

I loved how you introduced me as your sis,
I loved how our sunday roasts, you did not want to
    miss,
I loved how you and the Hubby did all that crazy shit,
We would laugh so much,
Our sides would metaphorically split.

But now i sit here with a broken heart,
As from this world you did part.
A single voice on the phone that day,
Made time stand still
And the world around me crumble away,
A world in which you shone so bright,
Loved by so many, now gone is your light.

As days turn to weeks and weeks to months,
the pain of loosing you still wont go away,
You were only thirty five Bro,
Why could you not stay?

Everywhere I go, of you there is an echo,
I still hear your laughter and "roll us a fag Gee"
Memories of the fun we had,
Visions I see.

My tears fall for you as much as they did before,
And when I think of you,
My heart breaks a little more.
Although I know you're at peace with Dad
And it's this that gets me through,
Nothing will spare me the pain little Bro
of how much I really miss you.

For my Unbiological Brother Steven "Stevey G" Gow

6-11-1988 – 19-10-2024

Forever 35

Much loved and Deeply missed

UNWRITTEN REALITY

When you open it up you can step inside,
It's a place to go when you want to hide,
To get away from all that's real,
To escape to whatever time and place you feel,
You can come and go as you please,
Leaving and returning with relative ease.

You're able to look on as others do their thing,
Engrossed in their lives and all they're doing,
Excitedly following the twists and turns,
The truth of the crimes, you soon will learn,
Star crossed lovers with challenging times,
Houses with ghosts and secrets to find.

You join them on their journeys, but they do not know,
You follow their lives, you go where they go,
You're the unwritten character they cannot see,
But wherever they are, that's where you'll be.

You cannot stay in this world forever,
You know this and it's ok,
But it's a nice little place to escape to,
For having time out and to just get away,
And when you find your day is quiet,
Or at night when you have some free time,
It's nice just to pick up where you left off,
In your world of ghosts, love and crime.

It's perfectly ok to escape sometimes,
But making memories with loved ones is best,
For these are the moments in reality,
That makes you feel truly blessed.

So, when you are ready to come back to you,
Closing the book is all you need to do,
With their lives frozen in time, until you visit once
    more,
It's time to come back to reality,
Facing all you've avoided before.
It's time to face your own challenges,
It's time to face your own ghosts,
It's time to feel the love through your family,
And to be reminded,
It's your story that matters most.

WHERE HAS THE FESTIVE SPIRIT GONE?

Fleeting memories of Christmases long ago,
Little moments, feeling the magic I once knew,
As a child, surrounded by family,
With decorations, Christmas films and turkey too.
Fun little gifts dear old Santa has left,
Spinning tops, wooden toys and a doll,
Mum and Dad had not much to spare,
But we didn't care, we loved it all.

But as time passes me by,
Can someone tell me please,
Where has the magic of Christmas gone?
Why is the festive spirit hiding from me?

As a woman, that magical feeling returns,
While celebrating the first of many,
With the man I love and family around,
The festive spirit spreads its joy in its plenty,
As a mum, passing down to my children,
Traditions old and new,
That feeling only Christmas brings,
Spreading joy and laughter too.

But as time passes me by,
Can someone tell me please,
Where has the magic of Christmas gone?
Why is the festive spirit leaving me?

As the leaves turn brown and the air grows cold,
We play Christmas songs and films from old,
We try desperately to hold on to that feeling,
But can feel it slipping away,
We tell stories of a night before Christmas,
Ghosts visiting through the night,
A man changed for the better in time for Christmas
    day.

But as time passes me by,
Can someone tell me please,
Where has the magic of Christmas gone?
Why has the festive spirit left me?

As the years go by, the magic fades,
No longer do people care about Christmas day,
Now a holiday so commercialised,
That festive feeling no longer enough,
Only interested in making money,
Or gifting the expensive stuff.
The world has forgotten, no longer does it care,
About the wonderful festive feeling,
That once was everywhere.

Please Christmas spirit, where have you gone,
With the magic you spread to the world?
Please come back to where you belong.
So many take your magic for granted,
But there are still some who care,
So please, when next Christmas comes round,
Promise that you will be there.

SHATTERED REFLECTION

She stands alone in her glass house
Shattering every window and door,
With each stone she throws, it's plain to see,
Her reflection is visible no more.

She points her finger but does not see
Three fingers all pointing right back,
The attention she seeks in the form of woe me,
Leaves others taking the flack.

Her friendship questioned, respect for her gone,
Her loyalty put to the test,
As she tramples on those she claimed to love
In her bid not to be second best.

Can she really not see what she claims them to be
Is the true reflection of her?
Or does she really believe in what she says,
So the truth becomes just a blur.

Insecurities blast through every pane
Reflecting off all who are close,
It's time to stop throwing the stones now,
Or she'll loose those who she loves the most.

FUNNY, NOT FUNNY

It's funny how there are those that will smile at you,
Will "love, understand" be "comforting and supportive",
They will "help you out" in times of bad
And "loving advice" they will give.

They don't care how loyal you are,
It's that caring facade they want you to see,
It reels you in, making them feel like family,
Worse, in some cases, family they will be.

It's funny how wonderful they are to your face,
Yet what they say behind your back is a laughable
    disgrace.
As little as only a year ago, you let it get you down,
All your trust gone, all motives questioned,
These people didn't just do a job on you,
They really went to town.
But time has passed and you have grown to be
    who you want to be,
The mental strength you now have, allows you to see
    things differently.

It's funny what they will say behind your back,
Bad mouthing, throwing insults and thinking you'll
    never know,
"I'm laughing because she's trying to be a good mum"
Yes she is, thanks for noticing,
Insults that make you look good, cheers girl, way to go.

It's funny what they will say behind your back
When they're really no better than you,
"She let you down, you can walk away, we'll look after
    you"
You couldn't even look after your own
When he did what he did, yet you stayed
And although he continued to "assert his authority"
    over them,
You married him, nice job, well played.

What's funniest of all is when they try to call you out
On your questionable parenting flaws,
Reminders of how worthless you made her feel
And wanting to take her right out the door.
You know the horrendous mistakes you've made,
The guilt of past behaviours burn deep,
You own them, are deeply sorry, have learned and will
    do better
But the burning guilt for your mistakes, you will keep.

They however, will never raise their hands
For all the bad they've said and done,
Lies they've told, the weight they've thrown around,
yet they can do no wrong.
They will easily pass judgement on others,
Thinking that they know it all,
Yet they will never own,
Their own questionable parenting flaws.

What's not funny is wanting to take yours
but gave up theirs for the partner they're now with,
Shouting at, and manhandling those that aren't their
    own,

I guess bullying kids in this manor, is the only way they
    can feel big.

It's not funny how they can say all these things,
Without really knowing what's true,
Not funny that they try to muddy your name,,
Spreading lies and their thoughts about you.

Now you ask yourself, stones thrown back and forth
What will it achieve? What good will it do?
You realise how far you've come and grown
That you've stopped caring what people think of you.

People come and go from your life
Because you have something to learn,
But your life is always made better
When the negative leave and do not return,
And once these lessons have been learned,
To include knowing genuine from fake,
You can continue on your journey
Knowing the same mistakes you won't make.

For the first time in forever, you finally feel free,
Surrounded by those who mean the world to you
You can finally start to enjoy life and do what makes
    you happy.
So why don't you grab the bull by the horns,
Live each day like it's your last,
Enjoy making memories with loved ones when you can,
Because it's funny how time goes so fast.

YOU WONT BEAT ME!

There's darkness all around,
I'm falling into the empty,
I can't find the ground.
Falling, nothing to hold onto,
nothing to catch me as i fall,
nothing but a thick black wall.
There's chaos in my head,
so much noise and confusion,
making me believe it's all very real,
not just an illusion,
Why wont it let me be?
When will I be free?

It intensifies paranoia,
It makes irrational thoughts seem rational,
It constantly lies but i believe it all,
"you're a failier, you're a joke, they're laughing at you,
he doesn't love you, nobody wants to know"
It goads and taunts until I finally fall.
It plants visions involving those I love most,
that show the most devistating events,
praying on that which I most fear,
it all seems so real and intense.
Why wont it let me be?
when will I be free?
So much going on in my head,
worries of all situations life brings.
Death, Betrayal, Family, The Future

and panic about even the little things.
I struggle for breath, there's pain in my chest,
the walls are closing in.
Tears roll down my face,
clutching my head, I scream and flip out,
I need to get out of this space,
but I can't move, what's happening to me?
each breath gets shorter, my chest gets tighter,
Why wont it let me be?
When will I be free?

No longer do I know where I am,
yet I feel a warm embrace,
"it's ok I've got ya, take slow deep breaths,
let's just walk around at a slow pace"
His voice is soothing, his hold feels safe,
with one foot in front of the other,
I find each breath becomes easier to take.
Back in the room but exhaustion's set in,
so I lay down and sleep for a while,
knowing those who choose to surround me with love,
each give me my strength and a smile.
I know I'll have my good days and bad
and may always wonder, will I ever be free?
But finding ways to cope,
with the support of those I love most,
I know that, Anxiety, you wont beat me!

WOULD BE BETTER

I look around, nothing feels real,
Everything in my life feels so surreal,
A heavy feeling deep inside,
A fear, sadness and loathing, I just want to hide.
So many voices screaming in my head,
Everything closing in, suffocating,
Maybe it would be better if I were dead.

"You're useless, you're nothing, you are no good,
Your body doesn't even work in the way that it should,
You make bad decisions and stupid mistakes,
You're pathetic with no backbone,
How much more can anyone take"
The voices are loud and rife in my head,
"You ruin lives and everything you touch"
Maybe it would be better if I were dead.

People say that suicide is a selfish way to go,
That I am just feeling sorry for myself
But what do these people really know?
In a room full of people who can't hear when I shout,
I'm in a deep dark hole and I can't climb out,
So consumed with all that I feel I've done wrong,
Thoughts of all the good in my life are all but gone,
I feel like I'm suffocating with nowhere to run,

My downward spiral has more than begun,
The voices are screaming again in my head,
"You won't be missed, nobody cares"
Maybe it would be better if I were dead.

A knife to the wrists, pills down the throat,
A belt hanging off the door,
I sit alone, now I know what to do,
Soon I will be no more.
I close my eyes, feel my life slipping away,
Not long now and it will all be ok..
But it isn't,
As i cast my eyes on a terrible sight,
A creature dancing around a campfire,
Laughing with such glee at my plight,
A haunting sight of this celebration,
For the way in which my life was taken.

All goes dark then I open my eyes,
Above me, someone who really does care,
With tears glistening in his eyes,
And a desperate fear in his stare,
Loved and worthy enough to be saved,
By this man, a new path is paved
He holds me tight as the tears flow,
Washing away the negativity,
No longer do I want to go.

Black holes may be deep but love is endless,
You're truly worth more than you think,
So never be afraid to reach out your hand,
When you feel like you're at the brink.

You're never alone, there is always someone,
Prepared to take your hand, listen and get you through,
So grab their hand and start your climb
And learn to believe in you.
Your strength will silence the negativity
Running riot inside your head,
And that's when you'll start to really believe
"It's better that I am not dead".

STRONGER TOGETHER

How the hell did i not see,
What was happening secretly,
I let them down, fooled by lies,
They suffered in silence,
As I missed their silent cries.
Red flags hidden behind "love and support"
I should have seen I should have fought,
So blind was I, I know I failed,
But it's the strength in them that should be hailed.
Fearing the unknown,
And what the future would hold,
They stood up regardless,
And the truth they told.
Relieved to be believed,
To know they're not on their own,
Whatever happens from here on in,
They don't have to do it alone.
When it came time to take the stand,
Their strength and courage shone through,
With a determination to make the world see,
What that animal did in fact do.
Judgement day, they made it through,
He is going away for a long time,
They stood up to him with all they had,
Now he will pay for his crimes.
There is still so much healing that needs to be done,

But they don't need to be strong forever,
Because we have their backs and one thing we've
    learned,
Is this family is stronger together.

HELPFUL NUMBERS

If you have been affected by any issues raised in any of these poems or you are struggling with anything else please do not be afraid to reach out there is always someone waiting to help.

MIND - 0300 102 1234

SUICIDE PREVENTION HELPLINE UK - 0800 689 5652

NATIONAL DOMESTIC ABUSE HELPLINE (England + Wales) - 0808 2000 247

BEREAVEMENT SUPPORT - 0800 090 2309

MISCARRIAGE ASSOCIATION - 01924 200 799

CHILDLINE - 0800 1111

RAPE CRISIS - 0808 500 2222

ALZHEIMERS SOCIETY DEMENTIA CONTACT SUPPORT LINE - 0333 150 3456

HUB OF HOPE - The Hub of Hope app can be found through Google, or through Google Play Store on android or the App Store on iphone.

HUB OF HOPE is the UKs largest mental health directory whether you want to find a service to help you or you want to support someone else who is struggling.

PEACE BY PIECE - Peace by Piece, who can be found on Facebook and Tiktok, are a spiritual group who work with tarot, mediumship and energy healing and have offered to donate their time to support those in need. Peace by Piece are NOT professional councilors however, they do offer a safe space for anyone struggling to reach out should they need to talk and where possible guide them towards the right kind of professional help. Peace by Piece have only one aim and that is to bring Peace, Hope, Love and Happiness to all.

Blessed be.

The informatiion on this page is mostly UK based but please wherever you are in the world, don't suffer in silence, reach out, there will always be someone to take your hand.

All information on this page was correct at time of publishing.

ABOUT THE AUTHOR

Ginnette "Gen" Elizabeth Bates was born in Carmarthen, U.K in 1979, at birth Gen wasn't given a middle name so added her own when she was old enough, however, she recently changed her middle name to Elizabeth in honour of her Nan who, although she never met, she feels a deep connection to.

Gen is the third of six children all of whom along with their parents settled in Shropshire in 1983 where Gen and her siblings spent their school years and later meeting their own partners and starting families.

Gen and her second husband have been happily married for 22 years, they moved back to Wales 14 years ago where they have been raising their three amazing children and are now watching their grandchildren grow up all too quickly. They also have four fur babies and consider them, not as pets but very important family members who are loved as much as the children. As a family, they have had many ups and downs, a lot of heartbreaking times and traumatic events that they wouldn't wish on anyone but there has also been a great deal more happy, fun and amazing times with many treasured memories to hold on to.

Gen loves to play darts, do latch hook projects, write and she loves to read, reading is her safe space, an array of places to go when she wants to escape reality. Her favourite poet is William Sharp who wrote "A crystal forest" and "universe" but she also loves the crime, thriller and supernatural genres.

When Gen is not doing the above, she loves to watch a bit of T.V, her favourite shows are 9.1.1, Supernatural, Charmed and the Walking Dead, her favourite movies are Armaggedon, Disneys Beauty & the Beast and the Harry Potter series but more than anything Gen loves spending time with her Husband, Children, Grandchildren and Furbabies because for Gen nothing is more important then her family.

www.ingramcontent.com/pod-product-compliance
Lightning Source LLC
Chambersburg PA
CBHW032029040426
42448CB00006B/775